# THE TOTAL CHURCH BODY WORKOUT

by
TOM S. LONG

(Mr. Long is also the author of *The Complete History of the Old Testament in Twenty Minutes*)

Single copies of plays are sold for *reading purpose only*. The copying or duplication of a play, or any part of a play, by hand or by any other process is an infringement of the copyright. Such infringement will be vigorously prosecuted.

BAKER'S PLAYS
Boston, Massachusetts 02111

*Western States Representative*
SAMUEL FRENCH, INC.
7623 Sunset Boulevard
Hollywood, CA 90046

*Canadian Representative*
SAMUEL FRENCH, LTD.
80 Richmond Street East
Toronto M5C 1P1 Canada

## NOTICE

This book is offered for sale at the price quoted only on the understanding that, if any additional copies of the whole or any part are necessary for its production, such additional copies will be purchased. The attention of all purchasers is directed to the following: This work is protected under the copyright laws of the United States of America, in the British Empire, including the Dominion of Canada, and all other countries adhering to the Universal Copyright Convention. Violations of the Copyright Law are punishable by fine or imprisonment, or both. The copying or duplication of this work or any part of this work, by hand or by any process, is an infringement of the copyright and will be vigorously prosecuted.

This play may not be produced by amateurs or professionals for public or private performance without first submitting application for performing rights. Royalties are due on all performances whether for charity or gain, or whether admission is charged or not. Since performance of this play without the payment of the royalty fee renders anybody participating liable to severe penalties imposed by the law, anybody acting in this play should be sure, before doing so, that the royalty fee has been paid. Professional rights, reading rights, radio broadcasting, television and all mechanical rights, etc. are strictly reserved. Application for performing rights should be made directly to BAKER'S PLAYS, Boston, MA. 02111.

Whenever the play is produced, the author's name must be carried in all publicity, advertising and programs. Also, the following notice must appear on all printed programs: "Produced by special arrangement with Baker's Plays, Boston, MA."

Amateur royalty (production fees) for plays in *The Total Church Body Workout* are $10.00 for the first performance and $10.00 for each repeat performance thereafter, subject to change, payable one week in advance of the production.

Copyright © 1979, 1981, 1982, 1987 by Tom S. Long

*Made in U.S.A.*
*All rights reserved*

**THE TOTAL CHURCH BODY WORKOUT**

# INTRODUCTION

The plays in this volume can be produced with a minimum of sets, props, and costumes. I know. I've been performing them regularly for several years with a traveling drama group called "Friends of the Groom." When we started, our major staging requirement was that everything had to fit in the back of a Chevette. Our set was four large black wooden boxes. Our costumes were blue jeans and red T-shirts.

Since those days, we've graduated to a station wagon with a roof rack, and we've learned a lot more about what's really needed to make a production work. We now wear khaki pants and black shirts, and our boxes are stained a natural walnut. It's a gift to be simple.

The material has been performed in all kinds of churches, on college campuses, at youth gatherings, and even on community theatre stages. It's flexible. We've had fun ignoring stage directions, playing male roles as female and female roles as male. We've played scenes written for six with five. We've even rewritten lines to keep them current and to accommodate them to each actor's natural speech patterns. About the only thing we haven't changed is our desire to perform as skillfully as we can, and to communicate the message of Christ in a way that moves people: usually to laughter, often to thought, and sometimes to a deeper faith.

I can't guess what your experience with these plays will be. I only hope you have as much joy and fellowship performing them as we have.

*Tom Long*

This work is dedicated to old Friends, far and near; and to Karen — my first and best of friends.

— TSL

All Biblical quotations are paraphrased from the revised standard edition of The Bible.

## TABLE OF CONTENTS

BODY TALK.................................7

THE WALL..................................21

ONE DAY AT A BUS STOP ....................33

CONFESSION SCENES........................45

UNLESS A SEED FALLS ......................69

COFFEE HOUR AT LAODICEA................85

# BODY TALK

---

CAUTION: Professionals and amateurs are hereby warned that BODY TALK, being fully protected under copyright laws of the United States of America, the British Empire, including the Dominion of Canada, and all other countries of the Copyright Union, is subject to a royalty charge. ALL RIGHTS ARE STRICTLY RESERVED. Amateurs may produce this play upon payment of a royalty fee of Ten Dollars in advance to Baker's Plays, Boston, MA 02111.

# BODY TALK

## CAST

| | |
|---|---|
| EARS | HANDS |
| HEAD | HEART |
| EYES | BLADDER |

*The stage is set with six sturdy chairs or boxes, arranged in two rows of three, one row behind the other. The CAST MEMBERS Enter and take their positions, sitting in the chairs facing the audience. From the audience viewpoint they appear, from left to right: Front row—HANDS, EYES, and BLADDER; back row—EARS, HEAD, and HEART. As soon as all are seated, they mime sleeping for several seconds.*

EARS. *(Waking suddenly and standing)* Wake up, wake up! We have an incoming word from the Lord! I repeat. Incoming word from the Lord. We have an incoming word from the Lord. I repeat. Incoming...

HEAD. *(Standing sleepily)* Alright, alright. Just a minute. This is church headquarters. All body systems report for duty, on the double.

EARS. *(Saluting)* Ears, reporting for duty, sir! *(EYES looks through binoculars which he wears around his neck)*

EYES. *(Saluting)* Eyes, reporting for duty, sir!

HANDS. *(Saluting)* Hands, reporting for duty, sir!

HEART. *(Standing and saluting)* Heart, reporting for duty, sir! *(HEART begins to thump his palm lightly on his chest in a heartbeat rhythm. He continues this "heartbeat" until the end of the scene)*

BLADDER. *(With noticeably less enthusiasm than the others)* Bladder, reporting for duty, sir.

HEAD. O.K. everybody, look alive.

EARS. You want my report now, sir?

HEAD. Hold on just a minute. Let's get our bearings first. Eyes, where are we?

EYES. *(Scanning through the binoculars)* Surroundings show a large area with group seating. We appear to be at a worship service, sir.

HEAD. Worship service? What am I doing...? Oh, well. Everybody relax, get comfortable. We're about to receive the peace and consolation of God's loving message to us.

ALL. *(Mumbling positive comments as they relax)* Great, Alright, etc.

HEAD. Alright Ears, lay it on us.

EARS. A new commandment I give to you, that you love one another, even as I have loved you. By this all men will know that you are my disciples, if you have love for one another. Greater love has no man than this, that he lays down his life for his friends.

HEAD. Well, that's a nice thought for the day isn't it. I move we thank Ears for her helpful contribution, and then get on with our regular business.

HANDS. Hear! Hear! *(ALL applaud politely)*

HEAD. Now then, what's next? *(BLADDER raises her hand)* Yes, Bladder.

BLADDER. I think we've been sitting in this pew too long. I say it's time we go somewhere.

ALL. *(Ad libbing)* Yeah, amen, etc.

HEAD. Alright, then, everybody on your feet. We're going right out through those front doors. *(HANDS, EYES, and BLADDER stand up. HEART, HEAD, and EARS stand on their chairs or boxes)* Nobody can say this church doesn't move forward when it has to. Eyes, keep me posted. Forward, march! Left, right, left, right. *(On "march" EACH BODY PART snaps to face a different direction and begins marching in place. They present a picture of organized chaos)*

EYES. Door to the outside is on our right.

HEAD. Right turn, march! *(THE BODY PARTS turn to face new directions and continue marching in place)*

EYES. Door to the outside is on our left.

HEAD. Left turn, march! *(THE PARTS again turn to new directions and march)*

EYES. Door to the outside is to the rear.

HEAD. To the rear, march! *(ALL turn again and march. As before, no two parts seem to be facing the same direction)*

EYES. We're out in the world now.

HEAD. Hold it! *(ALL stop. As EYES scans the audience with his binoculars, the OTHER PARTS also turn and look in the same direction as Eyes)*

EYES. Visual scan shows weeds, grass, and broken bottles. I think we just went backwards out the rear door into a vacant lot, sir. *(EVERYONE grumbles)*

HEAD. Alright, alright. Calm down. Listen, maybe we need to have a little business meeting first, and pick a direction.

EYES. Everybody knows where we're going.

ALL. *(Except HEAD, ad libbing agreement)* Yeah, sure, etc.

**Eyes.** We're all working on speaking in tongues and prophecy.

**Bladder.** Speaking in tongues?

**Hands.** I thought we were marching for justice and peace.

**Ears.** Justice and Peace? What about evangelism?

**Hands.** What about world hunger?

**Eyes.** What about Bible study?

**Bladder.** What about plumbing in the basement?

**Heart.** How about asking God? *(ALL turn to look at Heart)*

**Bladder.** Name dropper. *(ALL the parts begin arguing at the same time, ad libbing remarks about their favorite cause. The confusion builds until HEAD interrupts)*

**Head.** Order! I said order! *(ALL fall silent)* Now, a little simple discussion ought to be able to sort this out. I think the first thing we need to do is find out what we've *been* doing. That way we can uncover any problems, and we'll know what to do next. So can I have the reports from my standing subcomittees please?

**Ears.** Ears, reporting for evangelism.

**Head.** Go ahead, ears.

**Ears.** After carefully listening to the needs of the local community, we were able to mount a comprehensive program of outreach to potential new members.

**Head.** Fantastic. Can you give us the details?

**Ears.** Well, basically the program is this: we're putting little white cards in the pews, and anybody that shows up on Sunday can fill one out if they're interested.

**Head.** Uh...well, I guess it might catch on. Who's next? *(HANDS raises a hand)* Go ahead, Hands.

HANDS. Hands reporting for social outreach. I'm proud to report this year we've been a part of two extensive programs. We sent a representative to the special conference on poverty at the Downtown Hilton, and we organized the wine and cheese party to discuss the alcoholism problem.

BLADDER. *(Whispering to Eyes)* Somehow I think we're still missing something.

HEAD. O.K., that's under control. Who's next?

EYES. Eyes, reporting for renewal.

HEAD. Go ahead, eyes.

EYES. Well, I'm happy to say we're really doing great! I mean, we've got so many people prophesying and speaking in tongues, it just about knocks you senseless when you walk into a meeting. Of course, our goal is to have every church member speak in tongues by the end of May...

BLADDER. No way you're gonna get me blabbing that gibberish!

EYES. Are you gonna limit God's power?

BLADDER. I say an ounce of love is worth a pound of tongues! *(The OTHER PARTS join the argument, with everybody speaking at the same time. The ad libbed dispute quickly turns into a shouting match)*

HEAD. People, please! People!! *(They all fall silent)* Honestly, you people are giving me a migraine! Now there's some kind of problem we're not uncovering here. Is there somebody who hasn't reported yet?

BLADDER. *(Without any enthusiasm)* This is Bladder, reporting for fellowship. How come *I* get stuck with this every year?

EYES. I think we may have just uncovered a problem.

BLADDER. I'm tired of this job. I'm not even a part of this body.

HEAD. Now Bladder, that's not true. I mean, what could be more important than love and unity between Christian brothers and sisters?

BLADDER. Come on, nobody here cares about that. Let me do something important like...running the altar guild. *(If necessary, for altar guild substitute church activity that tends to be a "sacred cow", e.g. "running the bazaar", etc)*

ALL. *(Ad libbing disagreement)* No, That's not true, You can't do that, etc. *(While everyone else continues to talk at the same time, EYES looks through his binoculars at a distant point behind the left side of the audience. He has obviously spotted something)*

EYES. *(Interrupting the confusion)* Beep! Beep! Distant early warning. We have a figure approaching on the horizon. *(ALL lean forward and stare in the same direction as EYES)*

HEAD. Identify please.

EYES. Visual image is of a twentieth century individual.

HEAD. Secondary characteristics?

EYES. Appears uncertain, searching for meaning.

HEAD. Religious affiliation?

EYES. None visible.

HEAD. O.K., O.K. This is our big chance. We can really make an impression on this guy.

HEART. *(Suddenly getting excited with a corresponding increase in "heart rate")* Maybe we could show him how much we really love God. Or maybe we could show him how much we love each other. Or maybe we could even show him how much we even love him. I mean, if we really lay down our lives for each other and reach out to him, maybe...

HEAD. Heart...Heart! Calm down, take it easy. This is a man of the world we're dealing with here. I don't want you to get all goopy on the guy. Now we all got the skills and the gifts to really impress this guy. All we gotta do is show him our stuff. So on the count of three, everybody witness. Ready...one, two, three...witness! *(Immediately, HANDS, HEAD, EARS, EYES, and BLADDER look down at their feet and shield their eyes with one hand as though trying not to be seen. HEART looks hopefully in the direction of the individual on the horizon, watching with a welcoming smile as the imagined figure moves from Left to Right across his field of vision. When HEART'S gaze reaches the right side of the horizon, his smile gradually fades into a sadder expression, and his heart rate slows from its excited pace. It is obvious that the imagined individual has walked past the Body and departed. Hearing the slower heart rate, EYES looks up and peers through the binoculars in the direction the individual exited)*

EYES. Beep, beep! Figure is gone from visual field. *(HEAD, EARS, and BLADDER relax from their "witnessing" poses)*

HEAD. Alright, how'd we do?

EYES. I...I think the Mormons got him.

ALL. *(Ad libbing)* Awww, What do they got we don't, etc.

HEAD. Aw, don't worry about it. The socio-economic factors were probably all wrong anyway. I tell you what, we don't need this. You know what we need? We really need something to cheer us up—get us all pulling in the same direction. *(ALL ad lib agreement)* How about a song? You folks like to sing? *(ALL ad lib agreement again)* O.K., who's got an ear for music?

EARS. That's me. I know one. Good old number three ninety-six.

ALL. *(Ad libbing)* Yeah, Sure, etc.

EARS. Ready? *(She directs them to start singing)*

ALL. *(Singing)* The church's one foundation is... *(The HEART sings "Jesus Christ Her Lord" while each of the other BODY PARTS sings something different. e.g. "A Solid Outreach Program," "The Four Spiritual Laws," "A Good Strong Church Headquarters". The song continues in a confusion of conflicting ad libbed lyrics until HEAD stops it with a shout)*

HEAD. Wait a minute. Wait a minute! What are you people singing? You're messing up the whole song.

EYES. I'm not messing it up. I've seen those lyrics a thousand times.

EARS. You're blind. I heard what you were singing and it was wrong.

HANDS. Oh, come on. You were both wrong.

BLADDER. You should talk. *(Once again, all the BODY PARTS jump into the argument, talking at the same time. Everyone screams out accusations except HEART, who contributes to the bedlam by trying to be a peace maker. The argument builds until it is louder and more animated than any that have gone before)*

HEAD. Alright that's enough! *(Really shouting)* I said, shut up!! *(ALL fall silent)* Let's just get one thing straight right now. *I* am in charge here. And I don't care what you people wanna sing. From now on, when we sing that song, we're gonna sing it the way I tell you to sing it, and that's final!

BLADDER. Wait a minute. You may be the earthly head of this body, but you can't make me go against my gut feeling.

EYES. That's right, I'll sing it the way I see it.

EARS. Who says we gotta sing that song anyway?

ALL. *(Except HEAD, ad libbing)* Yeah! Right! etc. *(BLADDER steps away from the rest of the Body, and takes a stand Downstage Center, facing the audience)*

BLADDER. *(Singing with gusto)* Jesus loves me this I know, for the Bible tells me so, little ones... *(The OTHER BODY PARTS look on with a mixture of disgust and disapproval. The HANDS steps Downstage to stand beside the Bladder)*

HANDS. *(Trying to out-sing the Bladder)* We shall overcome, we shall overcome, we shall overcome some day... *(BLADDER turns to face Hands, and both continue singing harshly at one another. EYES steps between the two and adds his own song to the din)*

EYES. We are one in the Spirit, We are one in the Lord, We are one in the Spirit, we are...

EARS. *(Moving to the others, and singing loudly)* I love to hear the story, of unseen things about, of Jesus and his glory, or Jesus and...

HEAD. *(Singing over all the others)* A mighty fortress is our God. A bulwark never failing. Our helper he amid the flood... *(HEAD moves Downstage, and the HEART is left standing by himself on his chair or box as the others scream their songs at one another hatefully. The HEAD, HANDS, EARS, EYES, and BLADDER gradually move away from each other until they are spread out across the front of the audience. Each one finds his own spot where he can turn away from the others and continue singing. As soon as the parts are standing alone, however, they begin to look a little ill. Their voices grow weaker and more halting, and it's obvious they are losing energy. The HEART meanwhile has moved a few steps Downstage from his chair, and he watches the others with increasing concern. The first lines of Heart's speech are almost completely lost behind the singing of the others)*

HEART. No! Stop...you don't understand. There's only one head. We all have Christ's Spirit in us. Come on...if we're all really following Him...we have to work together...I mean if we all try and obey him... *(The OTHER BODY PARTS are really running down by this point. Each one slowly sags over from the waist, his voice and song slowing down and stopping like a record player that has been unplugged. For the first time, the audience can hear the Heart's lines over the singing. If necessary, HEART may need to ad lib extra lines so that the end of his speech corresponds to the dying of the other body parts)*

HEART. ...I mean...if we all just try to love each other...Hey you guys. Cut it out. You guys! *(The OTHER BODY PARTS are now completely silent and unmoving)*

HEART. If we just...lay down our lives for each other... *(The HEART now realizes that the others cannot hear him. He steps Forward slowly and reaches out to touch one of the Other Body Parts. There is no response. He looks over the five inert figures, and then sadly backs away Upstage a few steps. He pauses once more, and then with a brief gesture of resignation, HEART slumps forward like the others. The Six Figures hold their places silently for several seconds, and then HEAD straightens up from his position and speaks, no longer in character)*

HEAD. Just as the body is made up of many parts... *(As*

*HEAD speaks, the OTHER CAST MEMBERS also straighten up. During the following lines, ALL drift toward the Center of the stage where they stand in a comfortable group, facing the audience)*

EYES. ...and all the parts of the body, though many...

HEART. ...make up one single body...

BLADDER. ...so it is with the body of Christ.

EARS. ...For all of us...

EYES. Jews...

HEART. ...or Greeks...

HANDS. Slaves...

EARS. ...or free...

ALL. All have been baptized into one body, and all have been given one Spirit to drink.

## PRODUCTION NOTES:

The scene is based on I Corinthians 12:12-26.

This scene can be easily adapted for five performers, with the Head taking most of the lines currently assigned to the Hands, including the committee report delivered by Hands.

The scene can also be changed to fit different situations by giving Ears a different Bible verse to read on page 8. The lines for Bladder on page 11 can be rewritten as well, so that Bladder represents a part of the church most appropriate for the specific audience watching the scene. e.g. instead of fellowship, Bladder might report for Christian education or youth group or stewardship, still complaining, "How come I get stuck with this every year?"

# THE WALL

---

CAUTION: Professionals and amateurs are hereby warned that THE WALL, being fully protected under copyright laws of the United States of America, the British Empire, including the Dominion of Canada, and all other countries of the Copyright Union, is subject to a royalty charge. ALL RIGHTS ARE STRICTLY RESERVED. Amateurs may produce this play upon payment of a royalty fee of Ten Dollars in advance to Baker's Plays, Boston, MA 02111.

# THE WALL

## CAST
MAN *(Mime skills needed)*
FIRST PERSON
CONSCIENCE
SECOND PERSON

*All roles can be played by performers of either sex.*

*The scene begins with a MAN standing Centerstage, his back to the audience. He turns Downstage slowly and reaches out one hand to discover an invisible wall in front of him. Pressing both hands against it, he tests it and finds it solid. He reaches out, first left, then right, but the wall appears to stretch in a line across the stage between the man and the audience. He seems trapped behind an invisible barrier. Finally he presses against the wall with his whole body. At this point the FIRST PERSON Enters from Stage Left, leading the CONSCIENCE on a leash. As they pass the trapped man, the CONSCIENCE notices him and stops to look.*

CONSCIENCE. Hey, wait a minute.
FIRST PERSON. What?
CONSCIENCE. Look at that guy in there.
FIRST PERSON. What about him?
CONSCIENCE. It looks like he's trapped or something.
FIRST PERSON. So.
CONSCIENCE. So don't you care?

FIRST PERSON. About what?

CONSCIENCE. About what happens to him.

FIRST PERSON. I don't even know the guy.

CONSCIENCE. What difference does that make?

FIRST PERSON. He probably has his own friends. He doesn't want some stranger barging in on him.

CONSCIENCE. *(Urging FIRST PERSON forward)* So introduce yourself.

FIRST PERSON. *(Crossing Left to get farther from the man)* Don't be ridiculous. There's a wall there.

CONSCIENCE. You're not even going to try?

FIRST PERSON. Hey, look, I didn't put that guy in there. You act like it's my fault.

CONSCIENCE. How do you know it isn't?

FIRST PERSON. What?

CONSCIENCE. How do you know you had nothing to do with that wall being there?

FIRST PERSON. That wall was there long before I got here.

CONSCIENCE. And as long as he stays behind it, there's plenty more room for you out here, right?

FIRST PERSON. Oh come on. I don't care if he comes out here. But he probably likes it in there. It's what he's used to. He wouldn't be happy out here.

CONSCIENCE. Did you ask him that?

FIRST PERSON. I'm not going to force myself on him. He has a right to be where he wants to be.

CONSCIENCE. Look, I'm not asking you to drag him out. I just think you should unlock the door and give him a chance to decide for himself. Is that too much to ask?

First Person. Oh, I don't know.

Conscience. Come on, just give it a try. *(CONSCIENCE pulls FIRST to the right, approaching the man. FIRST gets very close, and then steps hurriedly to Stage Right to get farther away)*

First Person. He looks so...different. What if he's dangerous or something?

Conscience. Look, you want to be safe or you want to help somebody?

First Person. I don't want to get hurt.

Conscience. That's obvious. *(FIRST looks back at the man and finally decides, begrudgingly, to do something)*

First Person. Oh, alright. *(FIRST begins investigating the invisible wall as SECOND PERSON enters)*

Second Person. What's going on here?

First Person. *(Startled and embarrassed)* Oh, I don't know. I was just seeing if I could help this guy out.

Second Person. *(Gesturing toward Conscience)* Are you letting this thing bother you again?

First Person. Yeah, I guess I am.

Conscience. Hey, you were really starting to do something...

First Person. *(To Conscience)* Would you shut up for a minute and let me handle this? *(To Second)* It just seemed like the guy needed some help.

Second Person. Hey look, I know this kind of thing is unfortunate, but what are you gonna do—get in there with the guy?

First Person. Well, I wasn't really gonna go that far.

Second Person. It could happen you know. You throw

away all your time and effort and before you know it, you're just like him.

CONSCIENCE. Would that be so terrible?

SECOND PERSON. It wouldn't do either of you any good.

FIRST PERSON. I guess not.

SECOND PERSON. *(Ushering FIRST Down Left)* I know. You have to feel sorry for people like this. I mean, I really admire somebody who can live like that. But you know there's plenty more where he came from.

FIRST PERSON. Maybe there's some kind of agency that handles this sort of thing.

CONSCIENCE. Come on. Don't back out now.

FIRST PERSON. I'm not backing out. I just thought if there's somebody better at this than I am, I'll write them a check or something and they'll take care of it.

CONSCIENCE. But you lose so much that way. *(SECOND Crosses to First's right, interposing himself between First and the Conscience)*

SECOND PERSON. He's right. The money never gets to the people who really need it. *(CONSCIENCE Crosses to First's left)*

CONSCIENCE. That's not what I meant! It's OK. Send money. But there's a lot more to it than that.

FIRST PERSON. Good grief. What else do you want?

CONSCIENCE. Just make some kind of contact. I mean, for your own sake.

FIRST PERSON. What's that supposed to mean.

CONSCIENCE. Well he's trapped in there, but that also means you're trapped out here.

SECOND PERSON. *(Pulling on First's right arm)* Are you

gonna let a load of guilt push you around like that? That's a terrible reason to do something—just because you feel guilty.

CONSCIENCE. *(Pulling on First's left arm)* That doesn't have to be the reason.

FIRST PERSON. This is so confusing.

SECOND PERSON. I wouldn't put up with that kind of treatment. Why should you feel bad? You had to struggle. Nobody ever gave you anything.

FIRST PERSON. That's true.

CONSCIENCE. *(Pulling harder)* But it doesn't have to be that way. You could...

FIRST PERSON. That's enough, just leave me alone for once. *(The argument builds quickly, with CONSCIENCE and FIRST both talking at the same time. The actors may need to ad lib additional lines to make the quarrel rise in volume and intensity)*

CONSCIENCE. But you were so close...

FIRST PERSON. Just get your hands off me...

CONSCIENCE. This is a chance for you to...

FIRST PERSON. *(Physically pushing CONSCIENCE away)* I said shut up! *(FIRST and CONSCIENCE glare at one another for a moment, and then FIRST turns to face Second)*

FIRST PERSON. I don't know. Sometimes he really gets me running around in circles. How do you ever handle yours? *(SECOND PERSON glances behind himself and smiles smugly)*

FIRST PERSON. Hey, you don't even have one.

SECOND PERSON. I wondered when you'd notice that. *(Taking FIRST PERSON by the arm and leading him Downstage Right)* Come here, it's really easy. Just repeat after me: Let

## THE WALL

George do it.

FIRST PERSON. That's all?

SECOND PERSON. Sure. Go ahead.

FIRST PERSON. Let George do it.

SECOND PERSON. Good. Now try this one: If he really tried, he could make it on his own.

FIRST PERSON. If he really tried, he could make it on his own. *(As FIRST says this line, he begins to wrap the leash around his hand. With each line he repeats, he wraps the leash one turn further)*

CONSCIENCE. *(Starting to feel the leash pull on his neck(* Hey, cut that out. *(The following list of words and phrases starts slowly and builds in speed and intensity. CONSCIENCE is pulled closer and closer to FIRST PERSON, and begins to choke on the rapidly shortening leash)*

SECOND PERSON. What good can one person do?

FIRST PERSON. What good can one person do?

SECOND PERSON. If I got him out, he'd probably just go right back in.

FIRST PERSON. If I got him out, he'd probably just go right back in.

SECOND PERSON. He doesn't really want my help.

FIRST PERSON. He doesn't really want my help.

SECOND PERSON. I have my own problems.

FIRST PERSON. I have my own problems.

SECOND PERSON. Wife and kids.

FIRST PERSON. Wife and kids.

SECOND PERSON. My family.

FIRST PERSON. My family.

SECOND PERSON. My home.

FIRST PERSON. My home.

# THE WALL  27

SECOND PERSON. My job.
FIRST PERSON. My job.
SECOND PERSON. My car.
FIRST PERSON. My car.
SECOND PERSON. My God.
FIRST PERSON. My God.
SECOND PERSON. My self.
FIRST PERSON. My self.
SECOND PERSON. And me.
FIRST PERSON. Me.
SECOND PERSON. Me.
FIRST PERSON. Me.
SECOND PERSON. Me.
FIRST PERSON. Me.

SECOND PERSON. Me, me, me, me, me, me, me, me, me, me.

FIRST PERSON. *(Starting at the third 'me' above)* Me, me, me, me, me, me, me, me, me, me, mememememe mememememememe............. *(SECOND PERSON cuts First off abruptly with a gesture)*

SECOND PERSON. Now—close your eyes, click your heels together, and repeat: There's no place like my place.

FIRST PERSON. *(Following instructions)* There's no place like my place.

SECOND PERSON. Again.

FIRST PERSON. There's no place like my place...There's no place like my place...There's no place like... *(FIRST PERSON suddenly sucks in a great breath of air, almost as though he has been plunged into ice cold water. At the same moment, the CONSCIENCE jerks into a rigid crucifixion pose with arms outstretched, and the leash unravels from First's hand. FIRST holds his breath for a moment, then releases it, opening his eyes and relaxing. He drops his end of the leash. After a long pause, FIRST and SECOND turn toward each other. The lines which follow are spoken without warmth—in fact, almost without expression, except for a slight snobbishness. The words are a caricature of meaningless "cocktail party" small-talk)*

FIRST PERSON. Thanks.
SECOND PERSON. Anytime.
FIRST PERSON. Nice weather.
SECOND PERSON. Yes.
FIRST PERSON. How's the wife and kids.
SECOND PERSON. Fine. Yours?
FIRST PERSON. Same. Peas porridge hot?
SECOND PERSON. Peas porridge cold.
FIRST PERSON. Peas porridge in the pot.
SECOND PERSON. One.
FIRST PERSON. Two.
SECOND PERSON. Three days old.
FIRST PERSON. Take care of yourself.
SECOND PERSON. You too. *(The shake hands mechanically and then continue to stand staring past each other blankly. The MAN behind the wall, who has been looking on in horror with his hands pressed against the invisible barrier, slowly moves sideways. Through careful mime, he establishes that the wall, which up till now appeared to separate him from the audience, actually bends Downstage toward First and Second. The "Caged Man" follows the wall and discovers that it now curves around First and Second, encircling them. He presses against it, but First and Second are*

*clearly trapped inside an invisible cage, and the "Caged Man" is revealed to be the one on the outside. He shakes his head in puzzlement, and then Exits freely down the Center Aisle, leaving FIRST, SECOND and the Crucified CONSCIENCE in a frozen tableau behind him)*

*(Alternate ending for those less skilled in mime: FIRST and SECOND shake hands and Exit to opposite sides of the stage. The "Caged Man" steps up to the wall and taps on it to try to get a response from the frozen Conscience. The CONSCIENCE remains rigid, and the MAN turns away in despair)*

# ONE DAY AT A BUS STOP

---

CAUTION: Professionals and amateurs are hereby warned that ONE DAY AT A BUS STOP, being fully protected under copyright laws of the United States of America, the British Empire, including the Dominion of Canada, and all other countries of the Copyright Union, is subject to a royalty charge. ALL RIGHTS ARE STRICTLY RESERVED. Amateurs may produce this play upon payment of a royalty fee of Ten Dollars in advance to Baker's Plays, Boston, MA 02111.

# ONE DAY AT A BUS STOP

## CAST
MAN
STRANGER

*NOTE: The character "Man" in this scene can be played by a man or a woman.*

*The stage is bare except for three chairs side by side, representing a bench. MAN Enters and moves to Centerstage. He mimes appropriate actions to establish that he is waiting at a bus stop, e.g. he checks his watch, glances Offstage Left as though looking down the street, etc. After a moment, the STRANGER Enters carrying a briefcase. He sets the case down beside the bench and then moves to stand beside MAN)*

STRANGER. You waiting for the bus?
MAN. Uh...yes I am.
STRANGER. It's gonna be late.
MAN. Is that right.
STRANGER. Yeah. It's supposed to get here at 7:30, but there's a traffic jam up on twenty-eight. A guy up there had a blow out.
MAN. Oh. Did you hear that on the radio?
STRANGER. No, I was there.
MAN. Oh.
STRANGER. Yeah, it's gonna be... *(Checking his watch)* twelve minutes late. It'll get here at 7:42.
MAN. Well, I hope you're right.

STRANGER. I always have been before.

MAN. Really? I've never seen you ride the bus before.

STRANGER. Oh, I'm not waiting for the bus.

MAN. You're not.

STRANGER. No. I'm waiting for you.

MAN. *(Suddenly a little nervous)* You're waiting for me.

STRANGER. Yeah. But I tell you, you don't make it too easy. You know I had to hold up a thundershower over eastern Indiana, blow up a brand new Firestone all-weather whitewall tire, and make a two-and-half mile traffic tie up just to get twelve minutes with you.

MAN. Listen, I don't think I know you.

STRANGER. Well, you do and you don't. That's kinda the problem. I'm Jesus of Nazareth.

MAN. You mean...Jesus.

STRANGER. Yeah.

MAN. Ah.

STRANGER. Didn't recognize me, did you?

MAN. Well, you just...look a little different than I expected.

STRANGER. Lot of people say that, first time they meet me. *(Man decides he is dealing with a "harmless crazy" type who needs a little help)*

MAN. You live around here?

STRANGER. Yeah, I do. Of course, I live pretty close to everywhere really.

MAN. You wouldn't happen to live in some kind of special place...I mean, like a home or a hospital or something?

STRANGER. Yeah, there too.

ONE DAY AT A BUS STOP 35

MAN. You think maybe some people might be worried about you right now. Maybe looking for you?

STRANGER. Boy, there's a whole crowd of people looking for me. But I guess I'm more worried about the folks that aren't looking for me, you know?

MAN. Look—maybe I can help you. What's the name of the place where you live?

STRANGER. Well like I said, I live just about everywhere—Chicago, Vladivostok, Wapakoneta, Cairo, Poughkeepsie, sunsets, moonshine, interstellar space...*(Pointing)* I live up there in that cloud...the one that's shaped like the left hindquarters of an elephant...I live in a tomb three days old, and in the shining glory of God's right hand.

MAN. *(After a pause)* That's nice.

STRANGER. The main thing is...*(He taps a finger on Man's chest)* I'm trying to live right in there. But that's the spot that's kinda giving me a tough time.

MAN. *(Pulling away)* Listen...*(Reaching in his pocket)* you look like you could use a cup of coffee. Why don't you go somewhere and treat yourself on me. *(He holds out a dollar bill)*

STRANGER. No, I couldn't.

MAN. Go ahead, take it.

STRANGER. No...I really don't think we have time, you know.

MAN. *(Putting the money back in his pocket)* O.K. Whatever you want.

STRANGER. I really just want to spend a few minutes with you.

MAN. Look, Mister...Jesus...whoever you are...I think

you need some special kind of help. I mean, I don't know what I can do for you.

STRANGER. How about just talking with me. Person to person. You can do that, can't you?

MAN. Yeah, O.K.

STRANGER. Thanks. It really means a lot to me...communicating with you.

MAN. Yeah. It means a lot to me too...communicating.

STRANGER. Great. *(The STRANGER leans forward expectantly, waiting for Man to say something. MAN nervously turns away to look for the bus. There is an awkward silence, in which MAN does his best to ignore the Stranger. The STRANGER, obviously rebuffed, thinks for a moment and then begins to whistle "Amazing Grace" hopefully, MAN fidgets, but still maintains his distance)*

STRANGER. *(Abruptly interrupting his own whistling)* Listen...do you have anything you want to tell me?

MAN. I don't think so.

STRANGER. That's pretty unusual. Most folks have something they want to talk to me about. Something they're having trouble with or something they want me to do for them.

MAN. Yeah, I guess I see what you mean.

STRANGER. You want anything?

MAN. No, I think I'm fine.

STRANGER. No really, you can ask me. I really like it when people ask me for things they need.

MAN. Is that right.

STRANGER. Yeah—come on. Why don't you ask me for something.

ONE DAY AT A BUS STOP 37

MAN. No, I couldn't do that.

STRANGER. Aw, come on. I really love this. Just give it a try.

MAN. I don't know.

STRANGER. Come on.

MAN. You want me to ask you for something?

STRANGER. Yeah, anything you want.

MAN. Anything.

STRANGER. Yeah.

MAN. *(Finally rising to the challenge)* Alright...I'd like about a thousand acres of California beach front property..

STRANGER. *(Smiling encouragingly)* Yes.

MAN. ...a private Swiss chalet ski resort...

STRANGER. Yes.

MAN. My own Lear jet...

STRANGER. Yes.

MAN. An unlimited bank account...

STRANGER. Yes.

MAN. Irresistable sex appeal, of course...

STRANGER. Yeah.

MAN. ...and all the time in the world.

STRANGER. Yes.

MAN. What's your answer to that?

STRANGER. *(Still smiling)* No.

MAN. *(Moving away)* It figures.

STRANGER. But thanks for asking. No, I was really kind of hoping you'd ask for something you really needed.

MAN. Like what?

STRANGER. How about five more minutes with me.

MAN. Boy, you're a regular Santa Claus aren't you?

STRANGER. Well, it doesn't have to be five minutes. We could make it the rest of your life if you like.

MAN. That's O.K.

STRANGER. That includes forgiveness, by the way.

MAN. *(Moving away to sit on the bench)* I'll think about it.

STRANGER. Would you be willing to take a shoe shine?

MAN. What?

STRANGER. A shoe shine. I'll shine your shoes for you.

MAN. You're kidding.

STRANGER. No, really. I've got all my stuff in my briefcase here. *(He opens the case and takes out a can of polish and a rag for shining)*

MAN. Aw, I don't believe this.

STRANGER. Look, I wanna be able to do something for you. Come on, just put your foot right here. *(He places the case in front of Man)*

MAN. You want to shine my shoes.

STRANGER. Yeah. Come on, just put your foot here. Please?

MAN. Whatever turns you on. *(He rests one foot on the case and the STRANGER starts to shine his shoe)* I still can't believe you're doing this.

STRANGER. Well, I used to wash feet, but it kinda went out of style.

MAN. I guess so.

STRANGER. Do you mind if I ask you a few questions?

MAN. Like what?

STRANGER. Well...do you ever feel lonely?

# ONE DAY AT A BUS STOP

MAN. Me? I don't have the time.

STRANGER. Well, sometimes you can feel lonely, and you don't even know that's what it is.

MAN. Well actually, I wouldn't mind being by myself once in a while.

STRANGER. No, I don't mean that kind of feeling. I mean...can you name five people in the world you're important to?

MAN. Five? I could name a hundred and five.

STRANGER. Really?

MAN. Yeah. Everybody at work, my boss, my wife, the bank, the IRS...

STRANGER. No, no...I mean five people who really care about you. You know...wanna be with you, wanna listen to you...maybe wanna give you something.

MAN. Well you didn't say that.

STRANGER. Five people who love you just the way you are, no questions asked.

MAN. I don't know.

STRANGER. Could you name three?

MAN. *(Standing up and moving away)* It's a ridiculous question.

STRANGER. Name one.

MAN. Listen, if you're looking for some kind of perfect love, you're in big trouble, cause you're not going to find it. You can't expect other people to love you like that. I mean, I could never love anybody like that.

STRANGER. I'm not asking you to.

MAN. Well what do you want then?

STRANGER. *I* want to love *you* like that.

MAN. Oh, good lord.

STRANGER. Amen.

MAN. You're really something else, you know it.

STRANGER. Well, I'm glad you noticed that much. Listen, I know you think I'm mentally ill.

MAN. I didn't say that.

STRANGER. It's O.K., I knew you would. I just want you to know that I'm here because you asked me here.

MAN. What?

STRANGER. You know, every morning you wake up and stare at the ceiling and you talk to me.

MAN. Now you are talking crazy.

STRANGER. Oh, I know you haven't said more than three or four real prayers since you were little, but I still hear what you're thinking. You lie there, and what you're thinking is: O.K., things aren't so good right now, but just a few more days, a few more weeks, and I'll get on top of everything. When this rush is over...when I'm done with school, when I get the job, when the house is paid for, when the kids are grown...that's when things'll be good. But way down inside, your heart—your heart's saying: "Oh my God, that's the same thing I said to myself last year. I will *never* get there on my own." And that's why I'm here. I'm answering your prayer, Mark. *(Substitute real name of actor playing Man. MAN, who has been lost in thought as a result of the Stranger's words, suddenly comes to himself)*

MAN. How did you know my name?

STRANGER. *(Looking past man)* Hey, I think that's your bus coming. *(He moves quickly to his briefcase and replaces the shoeshine equipment)* Do you have the time?

MAN. What?

STRANGER. The time. What time is it, quick.

## ONE DAY AT A BUS STOP 41

MAN. It's 7:42. But you didn't answer my question.

STRANGER. That's O.K. I'll be around—really. *(He Exits Down the Center Aisle)* Be careful you don't miss your bus.

MAN. Yeah, right. *(MAN starts to move off to the Left toward the bus, and then glances at his watch)*

MAN. *(Stopping abruptly)* Hey. *(MAN looks up and stares in the direction that the Stranger exited. There is a touch of wonder in his expression. If no lights are available, the MAN should look for several seconds and then continue with an Exit to the Left)*

# CONFESSION SCENES

---

CAUTION: Professionals and amateurs are hereby warned that CONFESSION SCENES, being fully protected under copyright laws of the United States of America, the British Empire, including the Dominion of Canada, and all other countries of the Copyright Union, is subject to a royalty charge. ALL RIGHTS ARE STRICTLY RESERVED. Amateurs may produce this play upon payment of a royalty fee of Ten Dollars in advance to Baker's Plays, Boston, MA 02111.

# CONFESSION SCENES

*These scenes can accommodate a cast as large as fifteen or as small as three. Most of the scenes require only two or three performers, and only one scene requires as many as six. Small casts can easily leave this scene out when they select which material to perform. In many cases, the roles can be played by performers of either sex.*

SCENE #1: *Husband, Husband's Thoughts, Wife*
SCENE #2: *Teacher, Mr. Smith, Mr. Smith's Thoughts*
SCENE #3: *Checker, 1st Person, 2nd Person, 2nd Person's Thoughts, 2nd Checker, People waiting in line*
SCENE #4: *Mr. Sherman, Kim, Kim's Thoughts*
SCENE #5: *Person, Person's Thoughts*
SCENE #6: *Husband, Husband's Thoughts, Wife, Child*
SCENE #7: *Person, Person's Thoughts*
SCENE #9: *Jennie, Karen, Karen's Thoughts, Tom*

*In the scenes which follow, ordinary people are revealed in the middle of committing ordinary sins. The "Sinner" in each scene is accompanied by his thoughts which trail behind him on the end of a leash. At the end of each scene, when the act of sin becomes obvious, the audience hears a chime from offstage (Possibly sounded on a triangle) and the cast freeze for several seconds. Following the freeze, the performers relax and look toward the sinner, who "confesses" the sin to the audience. The rest of the cast respond with the words, "Lord, forgive us," and then join in singing a short Kyrie as they set up for the next confession scene.*

NARRATOR. *(To audience)* In the scenes which follow, the person wearing this leash represents the thoughts of the person holding the leash.

*(The CAST members for the first scene enter. The NARRATOR gives the leash to the actor playing the "SINNER" in the scene and exits. The SINNER puts the leash around the neck of his "THOUGHTS" and moves to his starting position)*

## SCENE #1. HEARTS THAT LIE

*(HUSBAND and WIFE sit side by side, facing the audience, watching television. The HUSBAND leans forward and mimes adjusting the picture to establish the presence of the TV set; he is clearly absorbed in the show. The husband's THOUGHTS stand behind him.)*

WIFE. Mark, could you go to the store and get me some sinus medicine?

THOUGHTS. Oh, no. Why is it always during the most exciting part of the show?

HUSBAND. Honey, do you think you could wait a little while?

WIFE. Well, my head's just starting to hurt. It'll only take a few minutes. You just have to run over to the drug store.

THOUGHTS. *(Disgusted)* Sure. Five minutes to get the car warmed up. Five minutes to the drug store... *(He suddenly thinks of something)* Hey ... wait a minute ... the drug store. That's right next to that ice cream place. You know, a hot fudge sundae would taste pretty good right now.

Peanuts, whipped cream, one of those little cherries. Boy, the more I think about it, the more I like it.

WIFE. Honey, for me...please?

HUSBAND. For you dear, I'd do anything.

WIFE. Oh, you're so sweet.

HUSBAND. It's easy when you really love somebody. *(He gets up and starts to Exit, with his THOUGHTS following)*

THOUGHTS. Or maybe a banana split! Yeah...in one of those plastic boats with two flavors of ice cream... yeah...and maybe some pineapple chunks and... *(The chime interrupts Thoughts. CAST freeze for several seconds, then relax and look toward Husband)*

HUSBAND. For the heart that lies, and the will that serves only itself...

ALL. Lord, forgive us. *(The CAST begin to sing the kyrie as they set up for the second scene, exchanging the leash if necessary and moving chairs or blocks around to create the next setting)*

ALL. *(Singing)*
Lord have mercy,
Christ have mercy,
Lord have mercy.

## SCENE #2 HANDS THAT STEAL

*(TEACHER is seated. MR. SMITH Enters with his THOUGHTS on the leash and moves to a spot representing the door to a classroom)*

MR. SMITH. Hello...Ms. Jones?

TEACHER. Come on in Mr. Smith. Have a seat. I'm

really glad you could make it.

Mr. Smith. Well, I like to keep up on how my kids are doing in school.

Thoughts. I hate these parent-teacher conferences.

Teacher. Well actually, Mr. Smith, I'm afraid we've been having a few problems with your son, Jerry.

Mr. Smith. Problems?

Thoughts. Oh no. He's not doing his schoolwork again.

Mr. Smith. Is it his grades?

Teacher. No, it's not that.

Thoughts. Thank heavens.

Teacher. I'm afraid Jerry's been taking things from the other students.

Mr. Smith. Taking things?

Teacher. Yes. Little things—pens, pencils, scissors. He's actually been going through the other students' desks to get them. We've caught him red-handed several times now.

Mr. Smith. Jerry, stealing? I can't believe it. Where would he get that kind of behavior from?

Thoughts. And pens and pencils of all things. I can get him all the pens and pencils he wants from the company where I work. *(Chime, CAST freeze, etc)*

Mr. Smith. For the hands that steal, and the actions that lead others astray...

All. Lord forgive us. *(ALL sing as they set up the next scene)*

Lord have mercy,
Christ have mercy,
Lord have mercy.

## SCENE #3 THE SPIRIT THAT IS QUICK TO JUDGE

*(The CAST stand as though in the checkout line at a grocery store. Downstage, at the front of the line, the CHECKOUT GIRL is ringing up the groceries of the First Person in line. Further back in the line stands a SECOND PERSON with her THOUGHTS behind her)*

CHECKER. Is this package of Twinkies yours, sir?

FIRST PERSON. Yeah.

CHECKER. How about the Pringles?

FIRST PERSON. Yeah, it's all mine.

THOUGHTS. *(Of the Second Person, observing the situation)* Look at that. Can you believe all that stuff?

CHECKER. Frozen pizza, canned sardines, bacon and onion dip...you must be having a party.

FIRST PERSON. Naw. Just my regular groceries.

THOUGHTS. What is this. This is supposed to be the express line. That guy must have twenty-five items there.

CHECKER. That'll be $75.37.

FIRST PERSON. *(Mimes searching through wallet for food stamps)* Just a minute. I got my stamps here somewhere.

THOUGHTS. You gotta be kidding. Food stamps! For that slop! That really burns me up. I work like an idiot day after day and I can't afford half that stuff. How can anybody be that selfish!

CHECKER. I'm not sure you can use food stamps for the Perrier water, sir.

THOUGHTS. Gimme, gimme, gimme! That's all those kind of people think about. Well there's takers and there's givers in this world, and right now the takers are walking all over us givers. *(A SECOND CHECKER Enters and steps to a position to one side of the First Checker, as though at another register)*

SECOND CHECKER. There's a new line over here. *(The SECOND PERSON and her THOUGHTS leap for the new line, clearly cutting in front of several people ahead of her, and even bodily elbowing one of them aside in her haste. The person who is shoved looks at her in surprise, but she only stares him down coldly, and plants herself at the front of the new line)*

SECOND PERSON. *(To Second Checker)* Well, it's about time. *(Chime, freeze, etc)* For the spirit that is quick to judge, and slow to sacrifice...

ALL. Lord, forgive us. *(ALL sing as they set up for the next scene)*

Lord have mercy,
Christ have mercy,
Lord have mercy.

## SCENE #4 EYES THAT DO NOT SEE

*(MR. SHERMAN, an old man, sits by himself on one side of the stage. KIM, followed by THOUGHTS, Enters from the opposite side and mimes knocking on Mr. Sherman's door. MR. SHERMAN gets up slowly and answers the knock)*

SHERMAN. Hello?

KIM. Hello, Mr. Sherman—I brought back the screwdriver I borrowed. Thanks a lot. *(KIM mimes handing Mr.*

*Sherman the borrowed tool)*

SHERMAN. Oh, thanks. Say, you wanna see something?

THOUGHTS. Oh no, not the parrot again.

KIM. Well...uh...

SHERMAN. Have you seen my bird?

KIM. Yes, I have.

THOUGHTS. Three times.

SHERMAN. He said a new word today.

KIM. *(Starting to edge away)* That's nice.

THOUGHTS. *(Tugging on the leash)* Get me out of here!

SHERMAN. I got something else here too. *(He turns away from Kim to look back into his apartment)*

KIM. I gotta go, Mr. Sherman.

THOUGHTS. *(Really pulling on the leash now)* Come on, move it!

KIM. *(Exiting)* Thanks again!

SHERMAN. It's a window. It's stuck. It's too heavy for me to lift. I thought maybe you could...uh... *(He turns back to the door and sees that Kim is gone)* ...well...I...I guess ...maybe not. *(Pause, chime, freeze, etc)*

KIM. For the eyes that do not see the needs of others...

ALL. Lord, forgive us. *(ALL sing as they set up for the next scene)*

Lord have mercy,
Christ have mercy,
Lord have mercy.

## SCENE #5 SELF PITY THAT RUNS OUR LIVES

*(PERSON Enters, yawning, with THOUGHTS trailing behind. From one side of the stage, someone shouts "Paper" and tosses a rolled newspaper to the front apron area of the stage. PERSON moves Downstage Center, faces the audience, and mimes opening a door. It is the front door of the Person's home, and the paper is lying on the porch in front of the door)*

PERSON. *(Cheerfully)* Good morning, God.

THOUGHTS. *(Drearily)* Good God, morning.

PERSON. *(Bending down to pick up the paper)* Well, let's see what's happening in the world today.

THOUGHTS. Same old story. Murder, crime, corruption...half the world starving to death... *(PERSON and THOUGHTS move Upstage. The PERSON sits and opens the paper and the THOUGHTS stand behind looking over the Person's shoulder)*

PERSON. Sometimes I wish I could do something...

THOUGHTS. What are you gonna do...send 'em your leftover breakfast in an envelope?

PERSON. I could send some money or something.

THOUGHTS. Oh, that's great. You're gonna throw money away down some rat hole with all the bills you got coming in this month?

PERSON. Yeah, I guess I should try to save a little.

THOUGHTS. Good luck. With the economy the way it is, you'll be lucky if you have a job next month.

PERSON. What *would* happen if I got laid off?

THOUGHTS. Yeah...the car is starting to sound funny again, this house is falling apart...

PERSON. Things are so depressing sometimes.

THOUGHTS. Things are depressing *most* of the time.

CONFESSION SCENES 53

PERSON. I feel so run down lately.

THOUGHTS. Run down isn't the word for it. You've spent half the year with a sore throat and some kind of flu. You've had a headache every day for the past month. And you never did get that blood test, did you.

PERSON. I really ought to do that.

THOUGHTS. It's probably too late by now. You always wait to the last minute to do everything.

PERSON. Yeah, it's probably too late by now.

THOUGHTS. What difference would it make anyhow?

PERSON. What difference would it make?

THOUGHTS. It's hopeless.

PERSON. It's hopeless.

THOUGHTS. Face it...

PERSON and THOUGHTS. *(Together)* My/your life is a mess! *(PERSON stands)*

PERSON. For the times we let self pity run out lives.

ALL. Lord, forgive us. *(ALL sings as they set up for the next scene)*

Lord have mercy,
Christ have mercy,
Lord have mercy.

## SCENE #6 THOUGHTS THAT KILL

*(HUSBAND and WIFE sit side by side as though in the front seat of a car. THOUGHTS stand directly behind Husband, who mimes driving. CHILD sits behind Mother as though in the rear seat of the car)*

HUSBAND. This traffic is ridiculous.

THOUGHTS. I swear, these family outings are driving me nuts. Rush here, rush there...If we had fun any more often it'd kill me!

CHILD. Mom, can we get popcorn at the movie?

WIFE. I don't know honey.

THOUGHTS. *(Noticing the car in front of him)* What is this? Where did this guy learn to drive? What an idiot!

WIFE. The movie starts in five minutes, dear.

HUSBAND. I'm going as fast as I can.

THOUGHTS. I'd like to see her drive in this traffic. *(Still looking at the car in front)* Oh great. So now the guy's gonna pull in. I guess the turn signals were optional on that model.

CHILD. *(Singing, to the tune of "Take Me Out To The Ballgame")*

Take me out to the movies,

Take me out to the show,

Buy me some popcorn and crackerjacks,

La, la, la, la, la, la, la, la, la, la...

*(The HUSBAND gives the Child a dirty look as the THOUGHTS chime in on the last line of the song, singing loudly over the child's "la's")*

THOUGHTS. *(Singing through clenched teeth)* If you don't shut up kid, you'll never get back!

WIFE. *(To Child)* Be quiet, honey. Your father's trying to drive.

THOUGHTS. We're never gonna make it.

HUSBAND. Keep your eye out for a parking space.

WIFE. There's one over there.

THOUGHTS. If this guy would move I could get to it. Come on, mister, move it!

WIFE. Is he stalled or something?

HUSBAND. I don't know.

THOUGHTS. I can't believe he's doing this. He's just sitting there. Come on buddy, we're waiting for the space!

HUSBAND. What's he doing?

THOUGHTS. Why don't you lean on the horn for a couple of minutes.

HUSBAND. Come on, make up your mind.

THOUGHTS. Better yet, why don't you roll foward and give him a little nudge...

WIFE. He's still sitting there.

THOUGHTS. *(Barely suppressed rage)* Even better...wait till he gets out and see if he can outrun your hood ornament!!

WIFE. Oh no...he's taking the space.

THOUGHTS. What! Aw, that's the last straw. *(Shouting)* Come on punk, make my day! *(THOUGHTS pulls out a blank gun, points it forward at the imaginary car, and fires it several times)*

WIFE. *(After a fairly lengthy pause)* Honey...wait a minute. Look who's getting out of that car...

THOUGHTS. Oh no...

HUSBAND. *(Rolling down the window)* Good evening... Reverend ___. *(Insert the name of the priest or minister of the church where the scene is being performed. Chime, freeze, etc)*

HUSBAND. For the thoughts that kill, and for the lives too busy to have time for you...

ALL. Lord, forgive us. *(ALL cast members from all the scenes step to the front of the stage and sing)*
Lord have mercy,

Christ have mercy,
Lord have mercy.
*(There is a short pause with all the CAST standing, facing the audience, then all exit)*

---

*OPTIONAL SCENES FOR CHRISTMAS SEASON:*

*SCENE #6 Can be modified to fit Advent by changing the lines as follows:*

HUSBAND. This traffic is ridiculous.

THOUGHTS. I swear, this Christmas rush gets worse every year. It's the national celebration of the invention of the cash register.

CHILD. Mom, are we gonna get to see Santa Claus?

WIFE. I don't know honey.

THOUGHTS. *(Noticing the car in front of him)* What is this? Where did this guy learn to drive? What an idiot!

WIFE. The store closes in fifteen minutes.

HUSBAND. I'm going as fast as I can.

THOUGHTS. I'd like to see her drive in this traffic. *(Still looking at the car in front)* Oh great. So now the guy's gonna pull in. I guess the turn signals were optional on that model.

CHILD. *(Singing, to the tune of "Santa Claus Is Coming To Town")*
Oh, you better not shout, you better not pout,
You better not cry, I'm telling you why,

La, la, la, la, la, la, la, la, la...

*(The HUSBAND gives the Child a dirty look as the THOUGHTS chime in on the last line of the song, singing loudly over the child's "la's")*

THOUGHTS. *(Singing through clenched teeth)* Santa's going to ring your little neck!

WIFE. *(To Child)* Be quiet, honey. Your father's trying to drive.

THOUGHTS. We're never gonna make it.

HUSBAND. Keep your eye out for a parking space.

WIFE. There's one over there.

THOUGHTS. If this guy would move I could get to it. Come on, mister, move it!

WIFE. Is he stalled or something?

HUSBAND. I don't know.

THOUGHTS. I can't believe he's doing this. He's just sitting there. Come on buddy, we're waiting for the space!

HUSBAND. What's he doing?

THOUGHTS. Why don't you lean on the horn for a couple of minutes.

HUSBAND. Come on, make up your mind.

THOUGHTS. Better yet, why don't you roll forward and give him a little nudge...

WIFE. He's still sitting there.

THOUGHTS. *(Barely suppressed rage)* Even better...wait till he gets out and see if he can outrun your hood ornament!!

WIFE. Oh no...he's taking the space.

THOUGHTS. What! Aw, that's the last straw. *(Shouting)* Come on punk, make my day! *(THOUGHTS pulls out a blank gun, points it forward at the imaginary car, and fires it several times)*

WIFE. *(After a fairly lengthy pause)* Honey...wait a minute. Look who's getting out of that car...

THOUGHTS. Oh no...

HUSBAND. *(Rolling down the window)* Good evening... Reverend __. *(Insert the name of the priest or minister of the church where the scene is being performed. Chime, freeze, etc)*

HUSBAND. For the thoughts that kill, and for the lives too busy to have time for you...

ALL. Lord, forgive us. *(All CAST members from all the scenes step to the front of the stage and sing)*
Lord have mercy,
Christ have mercy,
Lord have mercy.

## SCENE #7 FOR THE GIVING THAT KEEPS SCORE
*(Optional for Christmas)*

*(HUSBAND Enters with THOUGHTS on leash. He is leafing through the mail. His WIFE stands behind him making notations on a piece of paper)*

HUSBAND. Honey look, we got a Christmas card from the car dealer.

THOUGHTS. *(Reading over his shoulder)* "All my deepest love in this this season of joy and giving."?

WIFE. *(Crossing to stand beside him)* That's nice, dear. Listen, will you help me with the gift list?

HUSBAND. What's the problem?

WIFE. *(Showing him the list)* Well, I've got something for everybody in your family except your Aunt Edna.

HUSBAND. Do we have to get her something?

WIFE. She always gets us something.

THOUGHTS. Yeah, every year—another holiday assortment from the Cheese of the Month Club.

WIFE. How about a nice quilt for her bed?

THOUGHTS. Oh come on...That's gonna be forty bucks at least. I mean, how much does that cheese cost her?

HUSBAND. Uh...I think she's got one already.

WIFE. Well, how about bath towels?

THOUGHTS. Bath towels...Let's see, $5.00 each on sale...

HUSBAND. How many?

WIFE. I don't know. Maybe two or three. I can get them from that outlet store.

THOUGHTS. Three times five is fifteen...yeah, that cheese probably runs about fifteen bucks.

HUSBAND. Yeah, I think she'd really like that.

WIFE. *(Jotting it down)* O.K., good.

HUSBAND. What're you getting Jan and Bill Johnson?

WIFE. Oh, I already got them a set of those tupperware toothbrush holders.

THOUGHTS. Oh, tacky, tacky, tacky.

HUSBAND. Really?

WIFE. Honey, they're really practical. You know how much Jan and Bill travel.

THOUGHTS. Those things don't cost diddly squat.

HUSBAND. Are you sure, honey...I mean, last year they gave us that pewter tea set.

THOUGHTS. A hundred dollars, easy.

WIFE. Listen, there is no way I can compete with Jan Johnson, and I'm not even gonna try.

THOUGHTS. Yeah, but we don't have to embarrass ourselves.

HUSBAND. Honey, they've been our friends for a long time. Couldn't we find something a little more personal?

THOUGHTS. Something in the twenty to thirty dollar range anyway.

WIFE. I don't know.

THOUGHTS. I guess twenty would be O.K. if we throw in the tupperware on the side.

HUSBAND. I really think we ought to.

WIFE. Alright. I'll keep looking, but I don't have to like it.

HUSBAND. Come on, honey, don't talk like that. Remember, it's the thought that counts. *(Chime, freeze, etc)*

HUSBAND. For the giving that keeps score...

ALL. Lord, forgive us.

---

*OPTIONAL SCENES FOR YOUTH AUDIENCES*

## SCENE #8 SELF PITY THAT RUNS OUR LIVES
*(Youth Version)*

*(PERSON lies on three blocks or three chairs which represent a bed. Person's THOUGHTS stand behind her on the leash. Both are*

*asleep. Suddenly the sound of an alarm is heard. [This can be provided by two offstage actors making a discordant buzzing noise vocally.] PERSON wakes up, reaches out, and mimes shutting off the alarm. Then she sits up, stretching)*

PERSON. *(Cheerfully)* Good morning, God.

THOUGHTS. *(Drearily)* Good God, morning. *(PERSON gets up and moves Downstage to look in an imaginary mirror, facing toward the audience)*

PERSON. Well, I'm not looking too bad. Time to brush the teeth, wash the face—start out a brand new day.

THOUGHTS. Yeah, another crummy day at school.

PERSON. I got my English paper done. That's something.

THOUGHTS. You call that mess a paper? I've seen better papers on a roll in an outhouse.

PERSON. I guess I should've spent a little more time on it.

THOUGHTS. You always wait to the last minute to do everything.

PERSON. Well, at least I'll have a chance to see Mark again.

THOUGHTS. Yeah, you're gonna be a great hit with those zits all over your face.

PERSON. *(Touching face)* Gee, I hope he doesn't notice.

THOUGHTS. Doesn't notice? You look like you had accupuncture with a railroad spike.

PERSON. I really am breaking out.

THOUGHTS. And look at your figure. Are those your hips or did you stuff your jeans with a whoopee cushion?

Person. I'm so fat.

Thoughts. You'll look great hanging out of your basketball uniform tonight.

Person. Hey, there is a game after school. The coach said she might start me this week.

Thoughts. That was before the last game. You played like a moose on roller skates.

Person. Yeah, I'll probably end up on the bench all game.

Thoughts. As usual.

Person. I just feel so run down lately.

Thoughts. Yeah. And you got that stupid volunteer job at the hospital tomorrow.

Person. Oh, that's right.

Thoughts. Why don't you just bag it. You're not doing anybody any good.

Person. Yeah, I might as well stay at home.

Thoughts. Who cares anyway?

Person. Yeah, who cares.

Thoughts. You're worthless.

Person. I'm worthless...

Person and Thoughts. *(Together)* ...And stupid and ugly and clumsy and dumb.

Thoughts. You're a walking disaster. Face it...

Person and Thoughts. *(Together)* My/your life is a mess!

Person. I can't believe what a rotten day this has turned out to be after all. *(Chime, freeze, etc)*

Person. For the times we let self pity run our lives...

All. Lord, forgive us.

## SCENE #9 FOR THE TIMES WE DON'T STAND UP
*(For youth audience)*

*(KAREN Enters from Stage Right with her thoughts on the leash. JENNIE Enters from Stage Left)*

JENNIE. Hey, Karen, you gotta hear this. Do you know Ricky Frankenberger?

KAREN. Ricky Frankenberger?

KAREN'S THOUGHTS. Hey, maybe he's that new guy you thought was so cute.

KAREN. Did he just come into our English class?

JENNIE. Yeah, that's the one. Well, he just asked Beth Meyers to homecoming.

KAREN. Really.

THOUGHTS. Too bad. I guess she beat you to him.

JENNIE. That guy is so gross!

KAREN. Oh yeah?

THOUGHTS. Oh, my gosh, you almost admitted you liked him.

JENNIE. Oh, yeah! I mean the way he dresses. He looks like K-Mart threw up on him.

THOUGHTS. Better keep your mouth shut.

JENNIE. And talk about stupid! Yesterday, in history, Tom Peters asked him what he thought of MTV...

KAREN. Yeah?

JENNIE. Well old Franken-weiner says, "I don't know that much about sports, but my dad roots for OSU." Can

you believe that?
THOUGHTS. Don't just stand there...agree with her.
KAREN. That sounds pretty dumb.
JENNIE. Oh, yeah. I heard he spent some time in a mental hospital or something too. Seriously.
KAREN. Really? What for?
JENNIE. Who knows. He probably cut up a babysitter or something. I mean, isn't that weird?
KAREN. Well I guess so...
JENNIE. You *guess* so?
THOUGHTS. Come on, do you want her to think you're weird?
KAREN. Yeah, that's really crazy.
JENNIE. You're not kidding. Well, listen, I gotta run. See you.
KAREN. Bye. *(JENNIE runs off Right. KAREN watches her go. TOM Enters from the Left)*
TOM. Hey, Karen. How's it going.
KAREN. Oh, Tom. Hi. Hey, did you hear about that new guy...Ricky Frankenberger?
TOM. What about him?
KAREN. I just heard he was some king of mental case or something.
TOM. Who told you that?
KAREN. Jennie.
TOM. Oh Jennie. No wonder. Talk about mental cases.
THOUGHTS. Uh oh, be careful.
TOM. I mean if you could see inside that girl's head it'd be like, *(He mimics the Wendy's ad)* "Where's the brain. I don't think there's anybody in there."

KAREN. I guess you're right.

TOM. You didn't believe her did you?

THOUGHTS. Come on, you know what to do.

KAREN. No, of course not. Besides, I don't think it's right to talk about somebody behind their backs like she does. *(Chime, freeze, etc)*

KAREN. For the times we don't stand up for what we know is right...

ALL. Lord forgive us.

## PERFORMANCE NOTES:

You may wish to teach the kyrie to the audience prior to the scenes and ask them to join with the cast when it is sung between each scene. In most cases, when names are used in the script, it's best to substitute the real name of the performers playing these parts.

Performing all of the above scenes at one time is not recommended; the material is more effective if you select the five scenes which best fit your situation. For most church groups, scenes #1, #2, #4, #5, and #6 work well, in that order. For youth groups, a good series is #1, #8, #4, #9, and #6.

# UNLESS A SEED FALLS

---

CAUTION: Professionals and amateurs are hereby warned that UNLESS A SEED FALLS, being fully protected under copyright laws of the United States of America, the British Empire, including the Dominion of Canada, and all other countries of the Copyright Union, is subject to a royalty charge. ALL RIGHTS ARE STRICTLY RESERVED. Amateurs may produce this play upon payment of a royalty fee of Ten Dollars in advance to Baker's Plays, Boston, MA 02111.

# UNLESS A SEED FALLS

# CAST
SEED A — *Idealistic, and a bit naive*
SEEB B — *Self-centered, sure of his own superiority*

*The roles can be assigned to performers of either sex.*

*The scene begins with TWO ACTORS, playing TWO SEEDS, already on stage. Each ACTOR is crouched inside a large brown bag—burlap works well—with elastic sewn around the opening. The bags represent seed cases or shells. There is a moment of stillness before the seeds begin to grow out of the bags, slowly straightening and stretching until they reach their full height as plants. During their final stages of growth, the ACTORS simulate blooming by opening their hands and their eyes with accompanying popping noises. They respond to their surroundings with surprise and a touch of awe, since this is the first time the seeds—now plants—have seen the outside world. After several seconds of looking around, the two notice one another as their glances cross. They look away quickly and, in the brief embarrassed pause that follows, they arrange the elastic bag openings around their waists as if to make themselves more presentable. The bags are worn waist high—'sack race' style— until the end of the scene.*

SEED A. Uh...
SEED B. Yes?
SEED A. Uh, excuse me...
SEED B. Yeah?

SEED A. What are you? *(The two slowly lower their arms, dropping their plant poses)*

SEED B. Well, I...I was just about to ask you the same question.

SEED A. Me?

SEED B. Yeah.

SEED A. Can't you tell? Anybody could see I'm a seed.

SEED B. Oh really?

SEED A. Uh huh.

SEED B. Well, I'm Calvin Coolidge. *(Substitute the name of a celebrity or well known church figure)* Come on, what are you?

SEED A. I'm a seed. Haven't you ever seen a seed before?

SEED B. Look, you don't need to play any games. If anybody knows what a seed looks like, it's me. I mean, I ought to—I'm a seed myself.

SEED A. *You're* a seed?

SEED B. Of course.

SEED A. You're a *seed?*

SEED B. *(Irritated)* Yes, a seed. A propagative vegetable structure. The ripened, embryo-bearing ovule of a non-animal life form.

SEED A. *(With a good natured laugh)* Oh...oh, I get it. You're having a little fun. I mean, pretending you're a seed. It's a joke, right? I'm kinda slow I guess. We seeds are pretty thick sometimes.

SEED B. Hey, wait a minute! You, whatever you are, may not be too bright, but as a seed I take offense at that remark. And if you think you're amusing me by your

## UNLESS A SEED FALLS 71

infantile display of poor taste—I mean, you, insisting you're a seed...

SEED A. But I am a seed.

SEED B. Poppycrock!

SEED A. Poppycrock?

SEED B. You couldn't be.

SEED A. Always thought I was.

SEED B. Well you're wrong.

SEED A. I am?

SEED B. You are.

SEED A. Oh.

SEED B. Seeds are small.

SEED A. Yeah.

SEED B. Seeds are roundish and hard.

SEED A. Yeah. Yeah, that's me.

SEED B. No—look at yourself, you fool. Seeds have impenetrable outer casings. Like this... *(He makes a fist and strikes himself forcefully on the chest)* ...Uuuuuuhhhhhhhh!!

SEED A. You O.K.? *(SEED B, still gasping with pain, examines his chest)*

SEED B. What...what's wrong with me?

SEED A. I think you hit yourself.

SEED B. I'm...I'm all soft. What happened to my shell? *(He notices the bag farther down and grabs a handful of it)* Here...It's down here. And it's all broken up. *(SEED A leans over to look closer)* Don't stare at me. Why don't you gape at your own body. *(He sits and fingers the bag, almost in tears)* Oh, my poor beautiful body.

SEED A. *(Noticing his own 'casing')* Hey, now you mention it, I don't look so good either.

SEED B. *(To himself)* All cracked and torn.

SEED A. *(Investigating the elastic hole of his bag)* I've got a big hole right here in my forehead.

SEED B. *(To himself)* You never deserved this, you poor baby.

SEED A. And I'm coming out all over. *(SEED B sobs)* I don't feel that bad. In fact, I feel pretty good. *(He discovers his hands)* Hey, what are these things. They move. Wow. *(He shakes his hands, and then notices that he has taken a step forward)* Hey, this part moves too. Lemme see. *(He shakes each foot)* Right. Left. Right. Left. *(Starts to kick)* One. Two. One. Two. *(Begins jumping jacks)* One, two, one, two, one, two...Weeoo! Hey, come on up here and try this... *(SEED B gives a great sob for attention)* Hey are you alright? *(SEED B sobs even louder)* I guess it hurts a lot, huh?

SEED B. Ooohhhhhhhhhhhhhhhhhhh!

SEED A. *(Crossing to SEED B'S Right)* Is there something I can do?

SEED B. Oh, you don't understand. I was such a beautiful seed. So firm and strong. And look at this... *(SEED B continues to bawl like a baby)*

SEED A. *(Shouting over his crying)* Well gee...I mean...it's not that bad. I mean, look...I think you probably look better now than you did before. *(SEED B stops crying abruptly)*

SEED B. What?

SEED A. I said, I think you look better now than you did before.

SEED B. You think so?

SEED A. Well, yeah. Look. Before you were all brown and wrinkly and everything, weren't you?

SEED B. Yeah. That's true.

SEED A. And now you're nice and smooth and clean looking.

SEED B. I am a bit cleaner, aren't I. Yes.

SEED A. And before, you were on the short side... *(SEED A helps SEED B stand)* ...and now you're shooting right up there.

SEED B. Yes. Now that you mention it.

SEED A. And you're a better color...

SEED B. *(Beginning to bask in the flattery)* Yes.

SEED A. And more flexible...

SEED B. Yes.

SEED A. And much more lively looking...

SEED B. Yes, yes.

SEED A. And a lot stronger too, I bet.

SEED B. Oh, well...maybe just a little.

SEED A. All in all, I think you're a perfectly handsome, well developed...uh...well developed...plant!

SEED B. *(Moving Left)* Well, you have to expect quality when you start with quality, don't you? I mean, it's only natural that a seed like me would tend to improve in most circumstances. I really knew all along that good seeds make great...uh...great... *(He pauses to stare at SEED A)* What's a plant?

SEED A. Well, I'm not sure. It just sort of popped into my blossom. I think I remember hearing it somewhere.

SEED B. Hearing it?

SEED A. *(Drifting Right)* Now let me see...uh...I was lying down and some dirt was piled on top of me.

SEED B. Dirt?

SEED A. *(Beginning to remember)* Yeah. Yeah, we were

planted. It's coming back to me. First there was the dirt, and then there was the cow manure...

SEED B. What!?

SEED A. You know...the fertilizer.

SEED B. Fertilizer.

SEED A. Yeah.

SEED B. I certainly don't remember anything like that.

SEED A. It does seem awfully long ago.

SEED B. Well it can't be too important really.

SEED A. Oh, but yeah it was. And there was something else. I wish I could remember...

SEED B. *(Muttering to himself)* Cow manure, that's disgusting.

SEED A. There's gotta be somewhere you can get information about this kind of thing.

SEED B. *(Under his breath, sarcastically)* Why don't you look it up in your "Encyclopedia of Gardening."

SEED A. Hey, why don't I look it up in my "Encyclopedia of Gardening."! *(SEED A reaches down into the bottom of his bag and pulls out a garden manual. He begins to leaf through it as SEED B watches in amazement)*

SEED B. *(Crossing to SEED A'S Right)* Where did you get that?

SEED A. This? Oh, right here. *(He stretches his bag open so that SEED B can look down into it)* It's part of my chromosome structure. Genetic instructions and all that.

SEED B. Oh.

SEED A. Don't you have one?

SEED B. *(Trying to recover nonchalantly)* Uh...no. No, I

## UNLESS A SEED FALLS

really don't need that kind of thing.

SEED A. Boy, I sure do. *(SEED B steps away from SEED A as SEED A continues to look through the book. Trying not to be seen, SEED B worriedly checks out his own bag. To his horror, he finds that he too has a garden manual. He hurriedly stuffs it back into the bag before SEED A notices it)*

SEED A. *(Reading headings to himself)* "Compost Pile" ..."Soil Preparation"..."Garden Tools"...Here it is, "Planting Tips:" This common variety needs good soil and a great deal of attention. The truly devoted gardener will find that he needs to invest a great deal...

SEED B. Wait a minute. Did you just say "gardener"?

SEED A. Yeah. *(Pointing to a spot in the book)* It's right here. *(SEED B crosses to SEED A to look in the book)*

SEED B. Oh my Gardener, you're right. *(He starts to laugh)*

SEED A. What's so funny.

SEED B. *(Barely suppressing his snickers)* Oh nothing, nothing. Sorry. I shouldn't have interrupted you. Go on. Read the rest.

SEED A. Well, O.K. "The truly devoted gardener will find that he needs to invest a great deal of himself to keep these plants free from birds and choking weeds. The older plants are prone to crowd each other's territory..." *(SEED B has moved close to SEED A in order to read along with him, and in the process he has put his arm around SEED A'S shoulders. When SEED A reaches the line about crowding, he stops and glances nervously at SEED B'S hand which is resting on his shoulder. SEED B snatches his arm away and steps back, embarrassed)*

SEED A. "...with the hardier of the species robbing the

weaker of sunlight and nutrition. Since the young plants are difficult to distinguish from weeds, it is wise to mark the rows with a wooden stake and a seed packet. For illustration of mature plant with fruit, see diagram on packet." That's it!

SEED B. *(Affecting boredom)* What's it?

SEED A. *(Excitedly)* That's what I was trying to remember. There's a picture of what we're supposed to grow into!

SEED B. Is that right.

SEED A. *(Looking around)* Yeah, on a big wooden stake.

SEED B. You don't say. *(SEED A grabs SEED B'S arm and begins to pull him away)*

SEED A. Come on, come on. Help me look!

SEED B. Alright, that's enough! *(SEED A freezes. SEED B removes SEED A'S hand from his arm)* I have no desire to cross-pollinate with you.

SEED A. Sorry.

SEED B. Look, I hate to be the one to throw cold weed killer on your enthusiasm, but think for a minute. O.K., maybe there is a gardener and maybe we were planted. But what can you...what can any of us really know about all that?

SEED A. Well, I think...

SEED B. A few words in a garden manual? A vague feeling in your DNA?

SEED A. Well, maybe it's...

SEED B. Besides, don't you think if there is a gardener, he'd want us to stand up on our own taproots and decide for ourselves what we want to be. Instead of clinging to

# UNLESS A SEED FALLS

some old trellis about a stake at the end of the row. I mean that's a real nursery tale. *(Moving away from SEED A, with a little bit of a swagger)* No, I think it's up to each of us as responsible vegetables to grow our own way. You vine your way, and I'll vine mine. I mean it's not like we're mindless animals or something. We're strong, independent... *(During SEED B'S speech, SEED A glances down the center aisle and notices something in the distance behind the audience. It is the stake at the end of the row. He takes a step forward and squints)*

SEED A. *(Pointing suddenly)* Look! There it is! *(SEED B moves over to SEED A and stares for a long moment in disbelief)*

SEED B. *(Trying to recover from his embarrassment)* See, I...I knew if we just went about this calmly and rationally, we'd find the stake sooner or later.

SEED A. *(Still staring at the stake)* It's wonderful, isn't it.

SEED B. I don't know. I can hardly see it from here.

SEED A. Yeah, it is pretty far off. Just a minute. *(SEED A rummages in his bag and pulls out a pair of binoculars. SEED B watches in amazement)*

SEED B. *(To himself)* I won't ask. *(SEED A looks slowly up and down the stake with the binoculars, as SEED B waits impatiently)*

SEED A. *(Like a doctor checking out a patient with a stethoscope)* Uh huh.....uh huh.....uh huh..... *(Significantly)* Unnnnnnh...

SEED B. "Unnnnnnnnh"? What do you mean, "unnnnnnnnh"?

SEED A. *(Hesitant)* It's a picture of a plant alright.

SEED B. Well good. It looks like us then, right?

SEED A. Well, not exactly.

SEED B. How's that?

SEED A. *(Polishing the glasses on his sleeve)* It's...it's different somehow.

SEED B. You mean...we might not be done yet?

SEED A. *(Looking again and focusing)* I think... *(He gasps suddenly)* Oh!

SEED B. What's wrong?

SEED A. *(Still staring at the stake)* Oh no.

SEED B. It's not ugly is it? I don't want to grow ugly.

SEED A. Well...

SEED B. Come on, tell me. It's good looking, right?

SEED A. *(With reservation)* Yeah.

SEED B. Alright then.

SEED A. It's even...beautiful. *(Lowers the binoculars and looks at SEED A)* But there's something else.

SEED B. What?

SEED A. It's got a nail through it.

SEED B. No.

SEED A. Holding it on the stake, you know.

SEED B. Oh no.

SEED A. And some of its branches have been...trimmed away.

SEED B. Trimmed? You mean... *(He makes a cutting motion across his throat)*

SEED A. Yeah.

SEED B. Oooooooooohhhhhhh!

SEED A. But it's O.K., really. It looks like it's healthier.

# UNLESS A SEED FALLS

SEED B. *(Almost moaning with panic)* My poor branches. And I just grew them.

SEED A. Really, getting cut like that might've been good for it.

SEED B. I don't want to be good. I want to keep my branches!

SEED A. But it must be a good thing. The plant in the picture looks happy.

SEED B. How can you tell at this distance? You couldn't tell a smile from a tomato beetle from this far away.

SEED A. No. The plant in the picture has...has got fruit. It's been trimmed and it grew fruit. Fruit's a good thing, isn't it?

SEED B. Fruit! Who needs fruit? I don't know about you, but I eat dirt and water.

SEED A. The gardener. The gardener probably likes fruit.

SEED B. *(Aggressively moving toward SEED A)* The gardener! I've just about had it with this gardener of yours. I mean, who is he supposed to be, anyway?

SEED A. Well he's...he's...

SEED B. He's what? Come on, give me another one of your clever little stories. *(Mocking)* The gardener planted us, the gardener fertilized us, the gardener left us a picture.

SEED A. But everything I told you is true.

SEED B. How do you know it's true? I suppose this gardener is a personal friend of yours?

SEED A. No. I mean not exactly, he...

SEED B. Face it, you're living in a fantasy world. Look, I

don't have to make up anything. Just look at the facts. If this gardener is real at all...he must be a sadist.

SEED A. No.

SEED B. Yeah, that's what he is. A bully.

SEED A. Stop, please...

SEED B. A vicious, sadistic bully.

SEED A. No, stop!

SEED B. Stop yourself! Look, I was happy just like I was as an ordinary seed. And then he has to come and wreck it all by piling a bunch of dirt on me. Well I played along...I split my shell...I grew for him. Is that enough? Noooo. Not for him. No, he's gotta leave some sick picture of a dismembered plant lying around to torture us. And that's probably not the end of it. He's probably on his way over here right now with a pair of hedge trimmers to finish off the job. Well, I'm not sticking around here! *(SEED B starts to move away toward the spot where he first grew at the beginning of the play)*

SEED A. *(Grabbing Seed B's arm)* What do you mean? Where're you going? *(SEED B jerks away from Seed A)*

SEED B. Back to where I came from, where else. *(SEED B starts to wriggle back into his bag)*

SEED A. No. Wait. You can't do that. I mean it looks bad, but really, a plant can't live in a shell. *(SEED A tries to restrain Seed B)*

SEED B. Get away from me, you sick stupid little weed! *(SEED B pushes Seed A away hard. SEED A stumbles backward and falls to the floor. SEED B advances toward Seed A)* You can stay and play the game if you like. *(SEED B punctuates his words by grabbing the bottom of Seed A's bag, pulling it off, and throwing it at Seed A)* But I won't cry any sap for you when you're lying next to the cheese in somebody's salad bar. Me, I'm getting out of here. *(SEED B moves back to his original spot, crouches down, and pulls the bag closed over his head)*

SEED A. *(Getting up)* Wait, stop. No! *(He moves over to Seed B and circles him)* Come on, cut it out. This isn't right. *(He shakes the bag but gets no response)* Please. Come on back out. *(Pause)* Please... *(Pause, quieter)* Don't do this... *(Long pause, quieter still)* Please... *(After one more long pause, SEED A realizes there is no hope. He steps back sadly, turns away from Seed B, and then notices his own crumpled bag. He walks over to it, and picks it up from the floor as though he is going to climb back into it. Suddenly, he pauses and looks up toward the stake. After a moment of consideration, he looks back at Seed B and then down at the bag in his hands. Slowly, he looks back toward the stake, and then straightens slightly, and deliberately releases his bag, letting it drop to the floor away from him. His decision made, he walks forward, exiting down the center aisle toward the stake)*

## PRODUCTION NOTES

When lights and a curtain are not available, the actors can enter and climb into their bags at the beginning of the play with their backs to the audience. Once in the bags, they should freeze for several seconds before starting the scene.

Two Bible passages which can be read before or after the scene, or used in discussing the scene are: John 12: 24-26 and John 15: 1-2.

# COFFEE HOUR AT LAODICEA

---

CAUTION: Professionals and amateurs are hereby warned that COFFEE HOUR AT LAODICEA, being fully protected under copyright laws of the United States of America, the British Empire, including the Dominion of Canada, and all other countries of the Copyright Union, is subject to a royalty charge. ALL RIGHTS ARE STRICTLY RESERVED. Amateurs may produce this play upon payment of a royalty fee of Ten Dollars in advance to Baker's Plays, Boston, MA 02111.

# COFFEE HOUR AT LAODICEA

## CAST

LYDIA — *Church member*
THADDEUS — *Church member*
ALEXANDER — *Church member*
RACHEL — *Church member*

TITUS — *A visitor*
STRANGER — *A derelict or bag lady*

*In most cases, the roles in the scene can be easily adapted for either male or female performers.*

*The stage is set with two easels or stepladders which can be used as easels — one on Stage Right, one on Stage Left. A CAST MEMBER enters and places a sign on the Stage Right easel which reads "Laodicea, 60 A.D.". She then Crosses Left to the second easel where she places a sign which reads, "Coffee Hour." The OTHER CAST MEMBERS Enter and begin miming a coffee hour after a worship service, ad libbing appropriate small talk. RACHEL is serving. LYDIA, ALEXANDER, and THADDEUS pick up cups and move Downstage. TITUS remains Upstage and chats with RACHEL at the serving area. When the scripted lines begin, TITUS and RACHEL continue to mime a conversation, providing a backdrop for the other characters.*

## COFFEE HOUR AT LAODICEA

*If so desired, the setting can be established with a spoken introduction instead of the signs. Also, real cups, saucers, spoons, and tea and coffee pots can be rolled in on a serving cart and used throughout the scene instead of miming the necessary props.*

LYDIA. The sermon today was a little weak if you ask me.

ALEX. Well, the first part was alright, but he really lost me when he started rambling on about that faith and works thing.

THAD. Yeah, I agree with you there.

LYDIA. If he'd just keep them a little shorter.

ALEX. Amen.

THAD. Well, thank God we're not Troations. I heard last week they had one of those missionary types preach ...uh...what's his name...I know you've heard of him...

ALEX. Paul?

THAD. Yeah, Paul. Well this guy holds a Saturday night worship service, which is bad enough, and then he starts preaching...and he won't stop. I mean, he preaches for three or four hours straight.

LYDIA. I guess if you like your religion in strong doses.

THAD. Well, here's the funny part. Some kid in the congregation is sitting in a window, and in the middle of the sermon—he falls asleep. Next thing you know...right out the window—three stories—splat! *(The THREE respond with appreciative groans)*

ALEX. Next time we get a sermon like today, maybe we

# COFFEE HOUR AT LAODICEA

ought to try that one.

LYDIA. I got a couple kids I'd love to volunteer.

ALEX. Hey, what did happen to the kid?

THAD. Well, what I hear is, Paul runs out and heals the kid...and then goes right on preaching!

ALEX and LYDIA. *(Ad libbing)* Oh, you're kidding, Really, etc.

LYDIA. Well, you know, it's a whole different culture up there in Troas. Those people really go in for that foursquare gospel stuff.

ALEX. Yeah. You know, Ruth and I were on vacation up there last year and it really is a different world. I mean the streets up there are just full of these homeless little Macedonian beggars. Breaks your heart. We had a couple of kids come up and just about steal the hubcaps right off the chariot while we were in it.

THAD. Well I'm sure for folks like that, a good strong dose of fundamental gospel is what they need to make it through. I'm just glad I'm part of a church where you don't have to assassinate your brains to be a member.
*(RACHEL leads TITUS Downstage to join the others)*

RACHEL. Hey everybody, I'd like you to meet Titus Justus. He just dropped in for worship this morning.
*(ALEX, LYDIA, AND THADDEUS greet Titus and introduce themselves)*

ALEX. So you've never been here before?

TITUS. This is my first time.

LYDIA. What do you think?

TITUS. Well it sure looks great. I mean, I love the building.

ALEX. Yeah, we kind of like it too.

THAD. It's actually a modified Greek design. Sort of a cross between the Parthenon and the Temple of Solomon.

TITUS. Oh, and those cushions on the pews are beautiful. Was that needlepoint done by hand?

RACHEL. Yes. And there's the face of a different apostle stitched on each one.

ALEX. It's a pleasure just to sit on them.

THAD. Personally, I just like the feeling of space. You know, the forty foot ceilings and all. It's almost like you can feel totally alone...even when the whole congregation's here. *(RACHEL moves to the serving area and mimes picking up the coffee pot)*

LYDIA. Of course, the grounds have never quite matched the building.

ALEX. Well now wait a minute. You know they're hiring a Babylonian landscape artist to redesign some of that.

LYDIA. Oh, I don't know. I think some of those guys are overrated. I mean, one hanging garden and they're famous for a thousand years. *(RACHEL refills Titus's cup)*

RACHEL. I wish they'd do something about that tacky "Praying Hands" wallpapyrus in the kitchen.

THAD. *(Crossing to the serving area to set his cup down)* I'm sure they'll get to it.

ALEX. By the way, what do you do, Titus?

TITUS. I'm an executive for J and F.

ALEX. Jerusalem Fig?

TITUS. Yeah. They just transferred me up here with my wife and kids.

ALEX. Great. That's a great company.

TITUS. They've been good to me.

RACHEL. Well, I'm sure you have a lot to contribute.

TITUS. I hope so.

ALEX. Have you heard the choir yet?

TITUS. No, not yet.

ALEX. Well, you're in for a treat. Our music director is a real pro. Summa cum laude from Temple University.

THAD. Yeah, and he just hired a fantastic Ethiopian eunuch for the Castrati section. I tell you, when that guy sings those new Latin hymns, it just about brings tears to my eyes.

LYDIA. I don't know. That avant-garde stuff is Greek to me.

RACHEL. Oh, don't let her put you off. They do a wonderful job with the traditional Hebrew psalms too.

TITUS. Are there any social outreach groups here?

THAD. *(Moving to stand beside Titus)* Well sure. The church has a very active social outreach program. Uh...what's the name of that group...Rachel?

RACHEL. Gosh, I can never remember.

THAD. Well, there's a group that does that sort of thing. I'm sure they'd love to have your wife volunteer if she's into that.

ALEX. Heck, there's even some Bible study groups. I mean, if your wife's interested.

LYDIA. Of course, nobody's pushing you. I mean, you don't have to do anything if you don't want. That's one nice thing.

THAD. Yeah, and I think another thing to consider if you're gonna be living in the area is the church is just a neat part of the community. *(From behind the audience a STRANGER appears dressed as a bag lady or derelict. She wanders down one of the side aisles toward the playing area, gawking at her surroundings)* I mean, in some places, when you join a Christian synagogue, you feel like you're about to get fed to the lions, you know. But here, we really stress being a part of the community. Fitting in. In fact, I don't really think there has to be any difference between a church member and anybody else.

TITUS. That's good to hear. *(By this point, the STRANGER is coming to the end of the aisle and is visible to the entire audience. She pauses to investigate a hymnal or something else she finds in this area)*

RACHEL. I hate to interrupt, but who is that person over there?

ALEX. I don't know. I've never seen her before.

THAD. Holy Caesar, look at that get-up.

LYDIA. She looks like she got her clothes from a camel outfitter.

RACHEL. Do you think she's safe?

THAD. Oh, we get somebody like that every couple of weeks. When you leave your doors open to everybody, you're bound to attract a few unwashed types.

LYDIA. I don't know. Is that a patch of dirt on her neck or leprosy? *(The OTHERS in the group snicker)*

THAD. Very funny.

RACHEL. Do you think somebody ought to talk to her?

THAD. One of the ushers maybe.

# COFFEE HOUR AT LAODICEA

LYDIA. She probably wants a handout.

ALEX. I'll go say something. *(The STRANGER has wandered closer to the main playing area and now stands in front of the left side of the audience. She is still engaged in investigating her surroundings when ALEX approaches her. RACHEL, LYDIA, THADDEUS, and TITUS—while keeping an eye on Alex and the Stranger—turn slightly to face one another, forming a closed group. The STRANGER, a street person, speaks with a halting simplicity)*

ALEX. Hello there. What brings you here today?

STRANGER. I just like to visit places where they talks about Jesus.

ALEX. You're a disciple of the Messiah then.

STRANGER. I love the Lord Jesus. He healed me, you know.

ALEX. Well that's good. I'm sure he did.

STRANGER. He can heal you too.

ALEX. I'm sure he can. Now listen, if you want something, you know you can always come back after the Sabbath is over and ask the minister.

STRANGER. I just want to talk about Jesus.

ALEX. Well, the minister'll be happy to do that for you too.

STRANGER. Those people there—do they love Jesus?

ALEX. Oh yes. Every one of them. Now how about you plan on coming back tomorrow to talk to somebody. Does that sound good?

STRANGER. I love Jesus.

ALEX. That's nice. You come back later. O.K.? *(ALEX takes the Stranger's arm and starts to help her toward the center aisle)*

STRANGER. Jesus is coming back later.

ALEX. That's right. God bless you now. *(He gives her a*

*little encouragement to move down the center aisle to the exit)* You keep warm and eat well, you hear. *(Thinking his problem is solved, ALEX turns Upstage to rejoin the others. The STRANGER suddenly turns back and takes hold of ALEX'S arm. confronting him with a childlike sincerity)*

STRANGER. Do you love Jesus?

ALEX. Uh...well, yeah...

STRANGER. He loves you, you know. *(ALEX is obviously uncomfortable under the Stranger's stare)*

ALEX. Uh...right...

STRANGER. *(After a pause)* I love you too. *(THEY both are silent for a long moment. ALEX cannot seem to take his eyes off the Stranger)*

ALEX. I think you better go. *(After another pause, the STRANGER slowly turns away, obviously disappointed)*

STRANGER. Guess I'll look for Jesus farther on. *(ALEX watches intently as the STRANGER Exits down the center aisle. The OTHERS, who have been eavesdropping, gather around him)*

THAD. Boy, that was a live one.

ALEX. Yeah.

LYDIA. Well, you sure got rid of her.

ALEX. *(Still looking after the Stranger)* Yeah...I guess I did.

THAD. Hey, are you O.K.?

ALEX. Yeah...just something about that woman...

LYDIA. What?

ALEX. I don't know, it bothered me somehow.

LYDIA. Hey, you did fine.

THAD. Yeah.

ALEX. *(Obviously still disturbed)* I guess you're right.

*(ALEX turns Upstage and Exits abruptly. the OTHERS are left looking at each other awkwardly)*

THAD. *(Trying to recover from an embarrassing moment)* Well, Titus...welcome aboard. Listen, I hope you won't let this little episode here scare you off. Like I said, it really doesn't happen very often.

TITUS. No...no, I think I'm gonna like it here.

THAD. Well great. Cause I'm sure we'll all be really glad to have you.

RACHEL and LYDIA. *(Ad libbing)* Yeah, Right, etc. *(ALL Exit)*

*(Optional ending: Instead of exiting, RACHEL, LYDIA, THADDEUS, and TITUS freeze, and a voice is heard reading the following passage: Revelation 3:14-16)*

VOICE. To the church of Laodicea I say this: I know what you have done. I know that you are neither cold nor hot. I would that you were one or the other, but because you are lukewarm, neither hot nor cold, I will spit you out of my mouth. *(ALL break from the freeze and Exit)*

## PRODUCTION NOTES.

A good discussion text for this scene is James 2:1-9 and 14-17.

The scene is written for six performers but can be played by more than six, simply by assigning the lines differently.

# WATCH AT THE WORLD'S END

## by PHILIP TURNER

## A Sequel to
## *Christ in the Concrete City*

### The Most Significant Passion Play of Our Time

### Narrator, 2 Men, 2 Women
### Bare Stage

Like its highly regarded predecessor, this easy to stage work is a dramatic meditation rather than a play. It attempts to put into visual form the mystery that is at the heart of the Gospel: How can the life and death of an obscure carpenter two thousand years ago in an odd corner of the Roman Empire be relevant to our lives now? For assuredly, if it is not relevant, we are the dupes of the biggest confidence trick ever played on the human race. *Watch at the World's End* is only different from its predecessor, so states the author, "Because I am different. Twenty-five years is a long time in a human life. I do not know that age makes a man wiser, but perhaps it makes him more diffident; more inclined to say 'look' and 'listen' rather than urging fellow mortals to particular action." The play, for want of a better term, is very compressed. The words matter. It can be performed in a great variety of ways and settings from a reading in the context of worship to a dramatic action on a conventional stage. Ideal for touring.

### ROYALTY, $20-$15